Acro Curriculum: SCIENCE for ages 5–6

A wide range of teachers' notes and photocopiable worksheets to address the needs of teachers and children in covering several aspects of the curriculum, while learning valuable concepts in science.

Across the Curriculum Science for ages 5–6

Contents

Across the Curriculum Science for ages 5–6

Contents

Page

We show possible curriculum links but we will not have thought of everything so you may like to add some of your own.

Literacy

Describing living things.
Words relating to senses:
sense, eye, sight, see,
ear, hearing, smell, nose,
touch, feel, etc.
Words for parts of the
body: leg, wing, arm,
beak, etc.
Living and non-living:
alive, living, not alive,
human, animal.
Words and phrases for
making comparisons:
like, similar to,
different from.

Art

Picture of themselves.

RE

Discussions about
growing and
getting older.

ICT

Database of features:
eye colour, hair colour, height.
Finding information.
Pictograms of eye colour, etc.
Representing information
graphically.

PE

Movement: Which
parts of the body are
we using to move?
Copy the movements
of animals,
birds and fish.

History

Pictures of people at
different ages –
put in order.

Ourselves

Geography

Visit to a farm to
compare young
animals with their
adults.

Numeracy

Making pictograms of eye colours.
Data in a chart:
eye colour, size of feet, size of
head, hair colour, height.
Charts showing food children eat.
Height in non-standard measures.
Sorting living and non-living.
Lining up in order of birth date.
Are the oldest the tallest?
Tall, taller, tallest (humans).
Short, shorter, shortest (hand).
Long, longer, longest (worms).

Worksheet 1 includes vocabulary regarding the senses in addition to words for parts of the face and hand. Ideally this activity would be carried out in a small group situation with support from an adult. Opportunities should be taken to discuss childrens' own eyes, ears, noses and hands and how these are used for sensing the world around us. Children can learn how important the eyes are by being asked to describe objects in a 'feely bag' – this makes an excellent speaking and listening activity.

Worksheet 2 covers vocabulary that could be used when describing a bird. We have drawn arrows to the tail, to both wings and to both legs but only to one eye as only one is visible in the picture. Children should be encouraged to discuss similarities and differences between birds and humans, and why these differences occur. As an extension of this activity, children could draw a dog or cat, then label as many parts of the body as they can – again, similarities between humans, birds and animals can be discussed. You may wish to take this even further by drawing a fish and discussing similarities and differences. Children will begin to gain an understanding that animals are adapted to their environment.

Worksheets 3 and 4 provide labelling sheets for parts of the human body. As all the labels would have made one sheet too crowded we have provided two, with some significant words appearing on both sheets.

Worksheet 5 shows a hand and invites children to draw round their own, then to label the longest and shortest fingers and the thumb. You may like to take the opportunity to compare the pictures and the real hands. Our picture shows a hand where the third finger is the longest, but for many people the second finger is longest. You could establish which is more common in your particular class.

Worksheets 6 and 7 are used together as a history activity associated with the scientific theme of 'ourselves'. The children are provided with the opportunity to sequence the story of a person's life, from babyhood to old age. They should be encouraged to understand that a human starts life as a baby, grows through childhood to become an adult and eventually reaches old age before dying.

Worksheets 8 and 9 should follow a class discussion regarding eye colour. Ask children to work in pairs to look at each other's eyes. Each child should decide what colour the other person's eyes are, choosing from green, blue, brown or grey. This data should be collected by the teacher, perhaps using a class list on the board. There will then be opportunities to discuss the questions: 'How many people have blue eyes?', etc. Children colour the appropriate number of eyes on Worksheet 8, then cut these out to stick on the pictogram on Worksheet 9.

Name: Date:

My senses

WORD BANK

eye	eyes	see
tongue	taste	ear
ears	hear	hand
touch	nose	smell

This is an _____.
I can _____ with my _____.

This is an _____.
I can _____ with my _____.

This is a _____.
I can _____ with my _____.

This is a _____.
I can _____ with my _____.

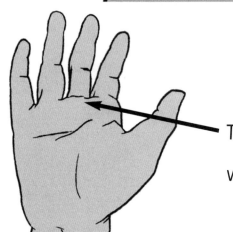

This is a _____. I can _____ with my _____.

Name: | Date:

Parts of a bird's body

The bird uses its _____ to _____ .

WORD BANK

leg   wing   eye

beak   fly   head

tail   wings

Name: Date:

Parts of the human body

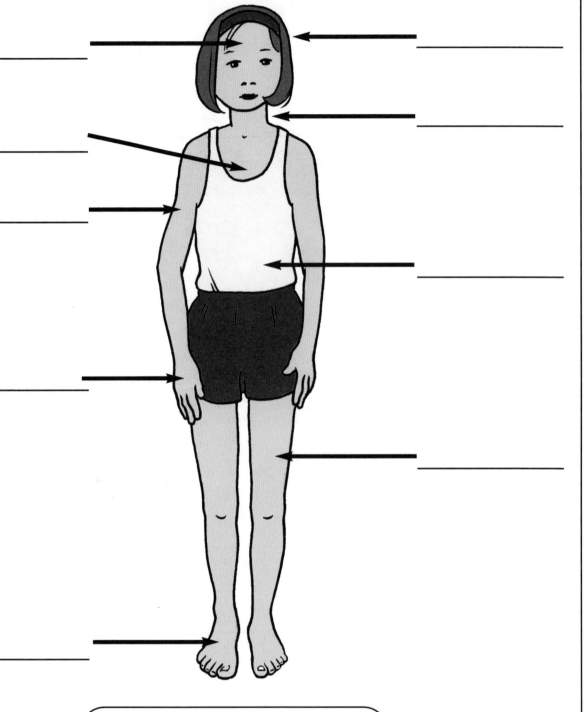

WORD BANK

arm	head	neck
chest	stomach	leg
hand	foot	hair

Name: Date:

Parts of the human body

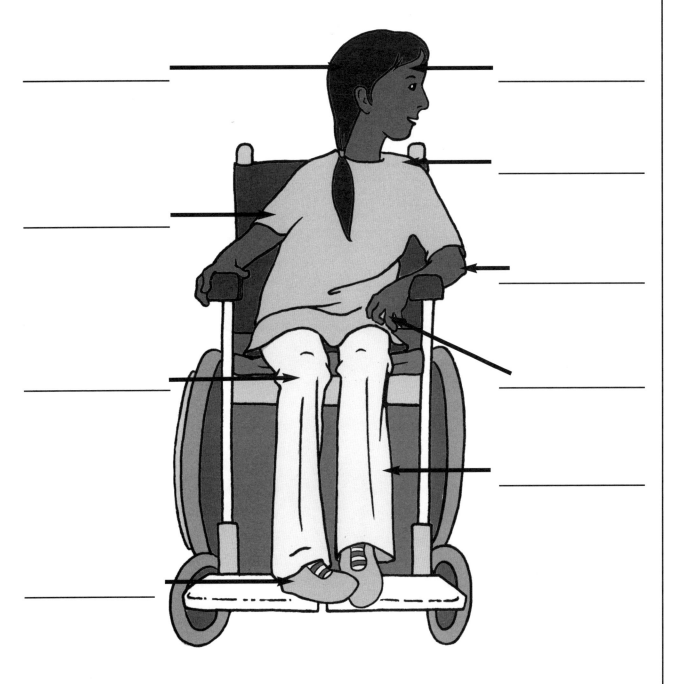

WORD BANK

leg	head	arm
knee	shoulder	foot
elbow	fingers	hair

Name: | Date:

Longest and shortest

longest

fingers

shortest

thumb

Draw around your hand.
Label the thumb.
Label the longest finger.
Label the shortest finger.

Andrew Brodie Publications © A & C Black Publishers Ltd.

Name: | Date:

The story of Jenny

Here are some pictures of Jenny.
They show her at different ages.

Cut them out and stick them on Worksheet 7 in the correct order.

Name: | Date:

The story of Jenny

1

Jenny was a
baby in 1930.

2

Jenny was a
schoolgirl in
1940.

3

Jenny got
married in 1950.

4

Jenny had
children.

5

Jenny is now a
happy old lady.

Name: Date:

Eye colours in our class

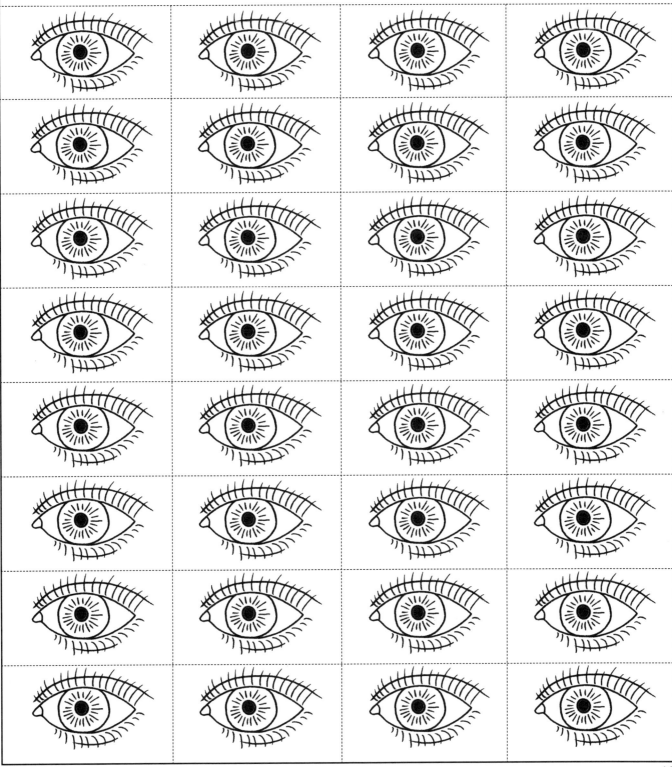

Iris – this is the coloured part.

Colour one eye for each person in the class. The eye should be the correct colour for the person.

pupil

Name: Date:

Eye colours in our class

Number of people				
Brown	Green	Blue	Grey	

Colours

We show possible curriculum links but we will not have thought of everything so you may like to add some of your own.

Literacy
Vocabulary: Words for making comparisons. (Could use Worksheet 5 from 'Ourselves'.) Words relating to plants, e.g. branch, flower, root, stem, seeds, seedlings, plants, leaf, weed. Name some common plants.

RE
Treating plants with care.

Art
Careful observation of one or two plants. Drawings of plants growing.

Geography
Walk around school, finding all the types of places where plants grow.

Growing Plants

Numeracy
Measuring heights of fast-growing plants (e.g. sunflower) using 'unifix' or similar plastic cubes. Chart of watered or not watered plants (e.g. cress, sunflower, bean). Keeping plants in light/dark:
– picture of plants at start
– picture of plants after 3 days
– picture of plants after 7 days
– picture of plants after 10 days.

Worksheet 1 lists vocabulary related to trees. Working with an adult, children select suitable words to fill the gaps in the two sentences provided. We suggest the following answers: 'The leaves are usually green. The trunk and the branches are usually brown or grey.' It would be very helpful to the children if you could take them out to look at a tree to discuss all the colours that they can see.

Children may need to be reminded that trees are plants. Many children view 'plants' as being flowers in pots or at the garden centre; they need to be encouraged to realise that the term 'plant' covers a whole range of living things, from a single cress to a giant oak.

Worksheet 2 shows a plant in a pot together with appropriate vocabulary to label it. You will need to have some plants in pots in the classroom so that each child can look at one carefully, then write a description of it with adult help.

Worksheet 3 provides a recording chart for measurements of a plant in the classroom. We have shown the measurement from the base of the pot as, of course, much of the plant is below the level of the top of the soil. Children may need reminding that plant roots are in the soil.

Worksheet 4 is a recording sheet for observations of two plants over several days, where one plant is provided with water and the other is not. With adult help, children can record what they observe in words or pictures. We classify this page as 'numeracy' as it is a simple representation in chart form.

Worksheets 5, 6 and 7 are used together to record what happens to a plant deprived of light compared to one that is kept in daylight. More able children will be able to write descriptions of what they observe; others should be encouraged to observe carefully and to verbalise what they see.

Worksheet 8 is a geography based sheet. Children are encouraged to walk around the school grounds, looking carefully and noting what plants they see. It is a good idea to ask them what plants they expect to see and where they expect to find them, before setting out on the walk – they may be quite surprised at how much plant life there is and where it is found.

Name: Date:

A tree is a plant

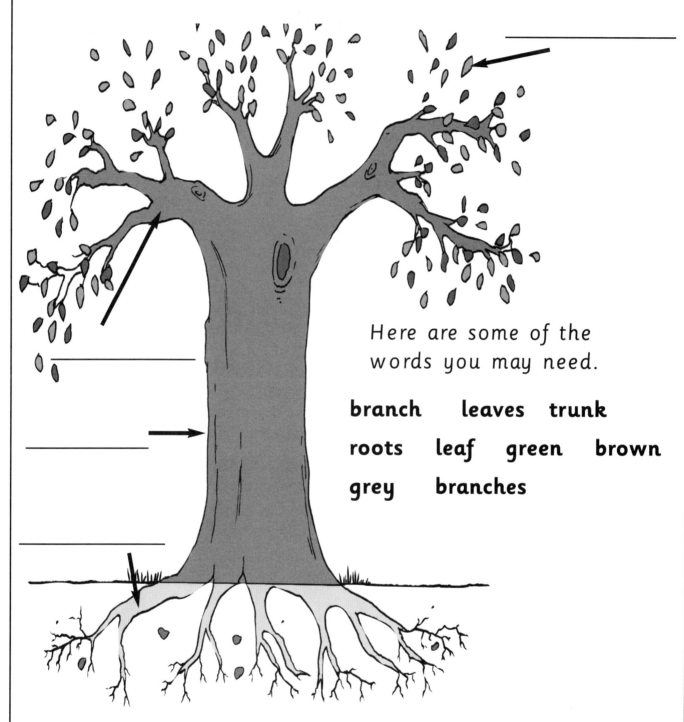

Here are some of the words you may need.

branch   leaves   trunk

roots   leaf   green   brown

grey   branches

Tree colours

The _____ are usually _____.

The _____ and the _____

are usually _____ or _____.

Name:

Date:

A plant in a pot

Practise writing the words you may need.

pot _____

leaf _____

stem _____

flower _____

roots _____

green _____

yellow _____

blue _____

red _____

orange _____

Describe one of the plants in your classroom.

_____

_____

_____

_____

_____

Name: Date:

Measuring a plant

This plant measures 17 plastic cubes in height.

It is 17 cubes tall.

Measure your plant every day.

	First week	Second week	Third week
Monday			
Tuesday			
Wednesday			
Thursday			
Friday			

Name: | Date:

Watering experiment

I am watering this plant every day.

I am not watering this plant at all.

What do you notice about the two plants?

	Plant with water	Plant without water
Day 1		
Day 3		
Day 5		

Name:

Date:

Light and dark

We are going to keep one plant in the dark ...

... and one plant in the daylight.

There is a plant in this dark cupboard.

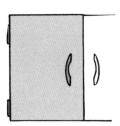

Here is a plant in daylight.

Draw both plants on day 1.

Name: | Date:

Light and dark

Plant in darkness | Plant in light

After 3 days

After 7 days

Describe the plants. _____

_____

_____

Name: Date:

Light and dark

Plant in darkness	Plant in light

After
10
days

After
14
days

Describe the plants. _____

_____

_____

Name: | Date:

A walk in the school grounds

Use your eyes.

Look carefully.

What plants can you see?

on the playground	
in pots	
by the fence	
on the field *grass*	
by the walls	
on the roof *the pond*	
reception gdn.	

Words you may need

grass   trees   daisies   weeds   none

We show possible curriculum links but we will not have thought of everything so you may like to add some of your own.

Literacy

Vocabulary: Names of materials: metal, plastic, wood, paper, glass, clay, rock, fabric, sand, china. Descriptive words: hard, soft, rough, smooth, shiny, dull magnetic, transparent, bendy, waterproof, strong. Comparisons: same as, different from, harder, smoother, etc. Use of feeling bags to encourage sense of touch. Writing to describe an object.

ICT

Creating a database of objects and materials.

Geography

Touring the school, finding objects made of different materials. What was the most common material?

Sorting and Using Materials

Art

Drawing, for example, a glass jar or a metal spoon.

DT

Materials can be named and described. Displays of objects: wooden objects, plastic objects, etc. Constructing a model home, incorporating appropriate materials for windows, doors, etc.

Numeracy

Drawing charts of objects sorted according to materials or attributes of materials.

Worksheet 1 lists vocabulary for commonly found materials. Children are encouraged to consider specific items and the materials they are made from. Adults working with groups could discuss why a particular item is made from a particular material and why it is not made from a different material. For example, the children could be asked why a fork is made from metal or plastic. Why is the fork not made from paper? Why are the pages of a book not made from metal? Which books have plastic pages and why?

Worksheet 2 shows a house with labels to complete. Some discussion will be needed, especially regarding what bricks or roof tiles are made from. Roof tiles are likely to be made from clay, concrete or slate and we have provided all three of these words at the top of the page. You may find it very helpful to take children out to look carefully at a house. Many children have never noticed a drainpipe. What is it for? What is it made from?

Worksheet 3 provides a range of vocabulary related to the topic, including specific materials and some of their properties. The vocabulary is practised using Worksheets 4, 5 and 6.

Worksheets 4, 5 and 6 are used together to create a fishing bingo game, for practise reading the words associated with the topic of sorting and using materials. The sheets should be copied onto card or paper that is then laminated. Each fish from Worksheet 4 should be cut out and have a paperclip attached. A fishing line is made, using a magnet for the 'hook'. The six bingo cards should be cut out. Within a group, one child is responsible for fishing words out and, with some help, reading them one at a time while the others are playing bingo with their cards.

Worksheet 7 is a geography based sheet. Children are encouraged to walk around the school grounds, looking carefully and finding objects made from specific materials.

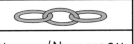
Name: Date:

Materials

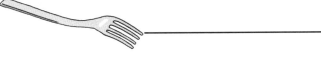

wood	paper	plastic	glass
metal	clay	fabric	sand

Write the material that each item is made from.

Draw another item made from the same material.

item   material   another item

 _____

 _____

 _____

Find some plastic things in your classroom.
Draw them on the back of the sheet.

Name: Date:

What is a house made from?

You may need these words: metal   glass   wood   plastic
slate   clay   concrete

Tiles are made
from _____ .

Bricks are made
from _____ .

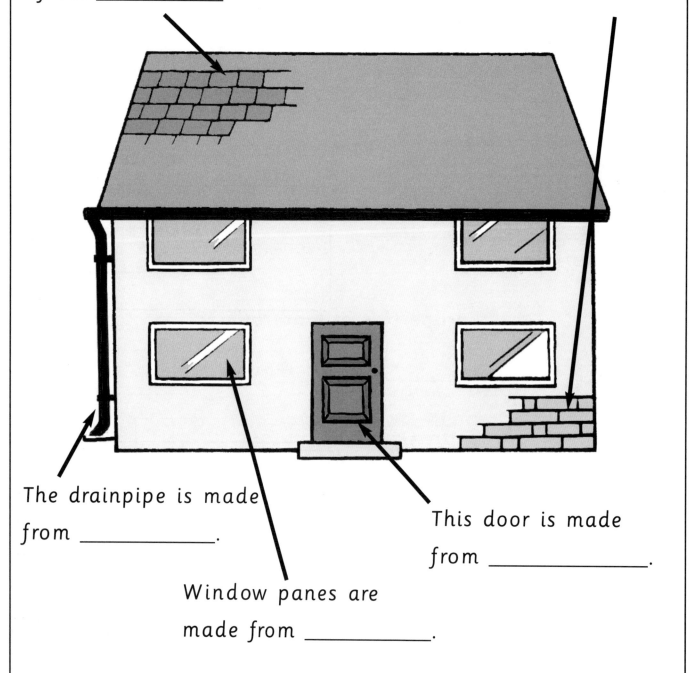

The drainpipe is made
from _____ .

This door is made
from _____ .

Window panes are
made from _____ .

What are <u>your</u> window frames made from?

_____

Name: | Date:

Materials and their properties

Practise the spellings.

materials

glass |

wood |

clay |

fabric |

sand |

metal |

plastic |

rock |

paper |

concrete |

properties of materials

hard |

soft |

transparent |

rough |

smooth |

shiny |

dull |

magnetic |

strong |

bendy |

waterproof |

Name: | Date:

Fishing bingo game

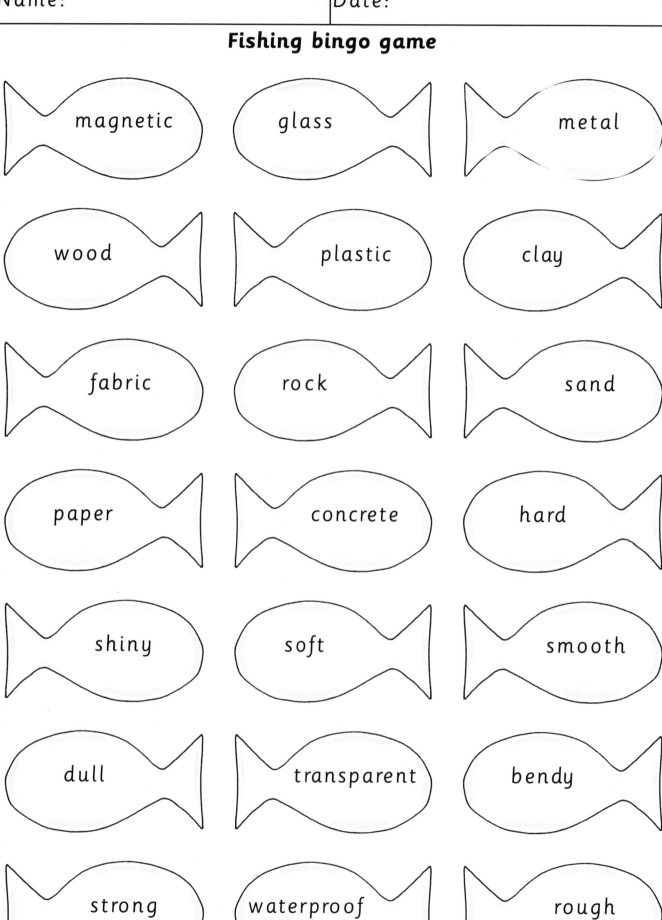

magnetic

glass

metal

wood

plastic

clay

fabric

rock

sand

paper

concrete

hard

shiny

soft

smooth

dull

transparent

bendy

strong

waterproof

rough

Fishing bingo game

glass		wood
	rock	
paper		fabric

	metal	
plastic	sand	clay
	concrete	

concrete		plastic
	glass	
metal		wood

Fishing bingo game

soft		magnetic
	dull	
rough		transparent

	smooth	
hard	waterproof	bendy
	shiny	

smooth		waterproof
	dull	
strong		bendy

Name: | Date:

Materials hunt

You are
going for a walk in
the school.

Try to find
two items made of
each material.

Draw or write the items.

glass

metal

wood

plastic

We show possible curriculum links but we will not have thought of everything so you may like to add some of your own.

Literacy

Technical vocabulary.
Vocabulary of comparison.
Comprehension of written instructions; captions, pictures.

ICT

Developing a word bank of technical vocabulary related to the theme.

RE

Lights in celebrations.

Light and Dark

Art
Shades of colour (lighter and darker).

Geography

Plan of home or school showing sources of light. See page 64 for a 'listening map' of a home.

Numeracy

Estimating numbers of objects up to 30, providing further opportunities for identifying light sources.

Worksheet 1 provides a range of vocabulary related to the theme of light and dark. The two captions at the foot of the page require children to read for meaning.

Worksheet 2 introduces further vocabulary, including the term 'light sources'.

Worksheet 3 contains a poem that provides information regarding day and night. This is followed by a comprehension exercise on Worksheet 4.

Worksheets 5 and 6 show light sources as a stimulus for estimation and counting exercises.
We suggest that the children write their estimate of the number of items shown in each picture in the box to the left of the picture, then actually count the items and enter this number in the box on the right. While the children work on this, opportunities should be taken to discuss repeatedly the vocabulary of light sources.

Worksheet 7 is designed for use on an OHP transparency but could be used as a laminated sheet in a small group situation. This gives an opportunity for an adult to read through a set of instructions with the children, as part of their reading comprehension activities for literacy.

Prepare for Worksheet 8 by providing three shiny items on the group's table. Again, the children will need to follow simple instructions. They may need some guidance to further their understanding of comparative adjectives. They will also need to fill in the simple chart, developing important skills for numeracy.

As an art activity, you may like to provide the children with a range of reflective papers and other materials. Sometimes it is possible to get hold of off-cuts of materials from which sequins have been cut. Children could then complete the following activity:

Look at the different papers you have been given. Choose the shiny papers to make a picture. Cut the shiny paper into interesting shapes to stick on your background. Shine a light on your picture. Does your picture reflect light?

Name: Date:

Wordsearch

On each row of the wordsearch below you will find three words. Write them on the lines.

m	o	o	n	d	a	r	k	b	r	i	g	h	t
▉	l	i	g	h	t	s	u	n	t	o	r	c	h
b	l	a	c	k	s	t	a	r	n	i	g	h	t
l	a	m	p	c	a	n	d	l	e	d	a	y	▉

_____   _____   _____

_____   _____   _____

_____   _____   _____

_____   _____   _____

Now draw and colour a picture to go in each box.
Read the captions first.

| The moon and stars look bright at night. | The sun gives us light in the daytime. |

Name: | Date:

Light sources

Look at the pictures.
They are all things that give us light.
These are called **light sources**.
Put the labels from the box under the correct picture.

WORD BANK

lamp	torch
fire	star
sun	candle

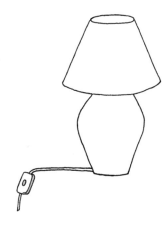

_____ _____ _____

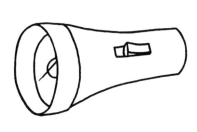

_____ _____ _____

Now colour the pictures. Use bright colours.

Name: Date:

Day and Night

By day I like the sun to shine,
And fill the world with light.
When darkness falls, the lamps go on
So we can see at night.

On sunny days I like to walk
Down lanes by fields of sheep.
But when night comes, I curl up in
My bed, and go to sleep.

All through the day when it is light
I see things far and near.
Then in the darkness of the night
Things seem to disappear.

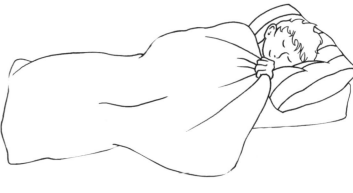

Now answer the questions on Worksheet 4.

Name: Date:

Day and night

Put a ring round the correct answers.

When the sun shines it is

night   light   fright

At night it is

dark   park   shark

What goes on at night to help you see?

banana   lamp   flower

In the poem, what do the fields have in them?

cows   horses   sheep

Draw lines to join up the rhyming words.

night   mine

day   light

sheep   stay

shine   red

bed   sleep

Name:

Date:

Estimation

How many items do you think are in each set?
Count them to see if you are right.

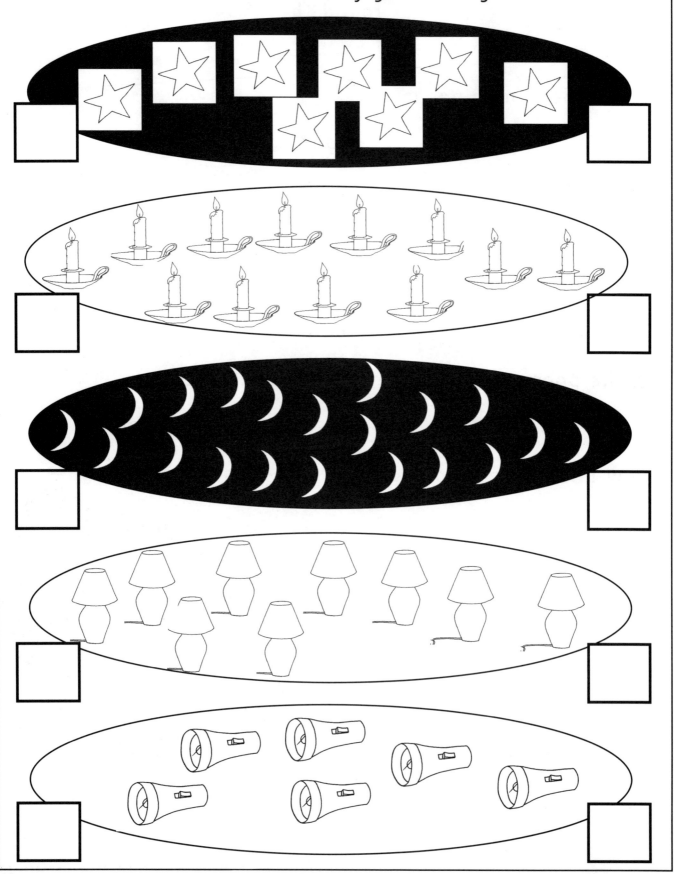

Name: Date:

Estimation

How many items do you think are in each set?
Count them to see if you are right.

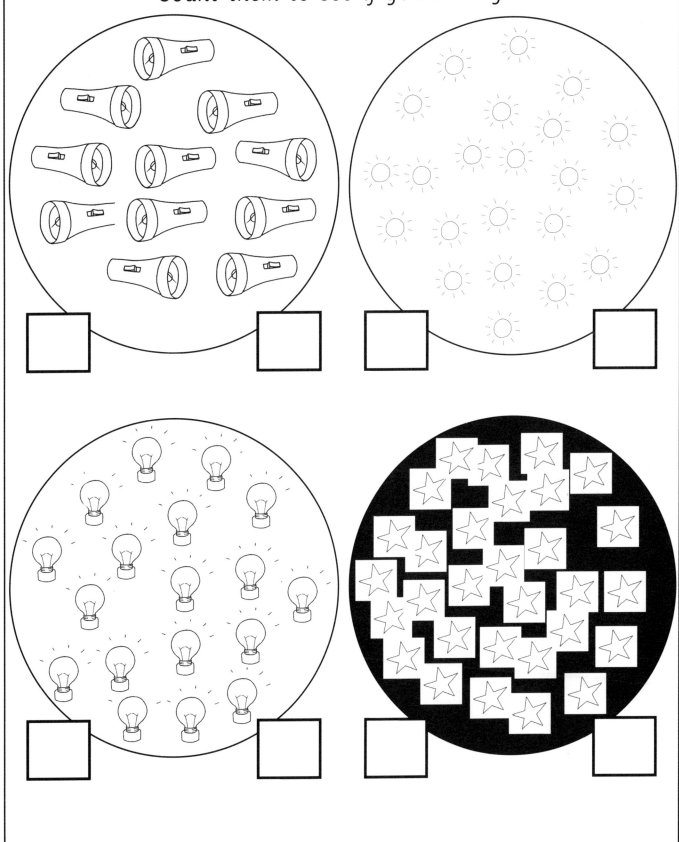

Andrew Brodie Publications © A & C Black Publishers Ltd.

Getting lighter and lighter

🖌 You have one piece of paper for painting on.

🖌 Choose one colour of paint.

🖌 You will also need to use white paint.

🖌 Paint a stripe of your colour at the top of the paper.

🖌 Add a <u>little</u> white paint to your colour.

🖌 Paint another stripe just below the first one.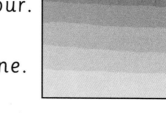

🖌 Add a little more white paint to your colour.

🖌 Paint another stripe just below the last one.

🖌 Carry on adding more white paint and painting more stripes until the paper is full.

🖌 <u>Variations</u>

Paint wiggly stripes.

Start with a colour and add black to get darker.

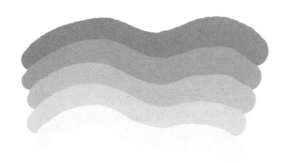

Name: Date:

Reflections

Some things **reflect** light.

Mirrors and water can **reflect** light.

All sorts of smooth shiny surfaces can **reflect** light.

Look at the shiny things on your table.

Decide which items are the best **reflectors**.

Put them in order.

Draw the items. Draw the best reflector first. Draw the worst reflector last.

best reflector   worst reflector

We show possible curriculum links but we will not have thought of everything so you may like to add some of your own.

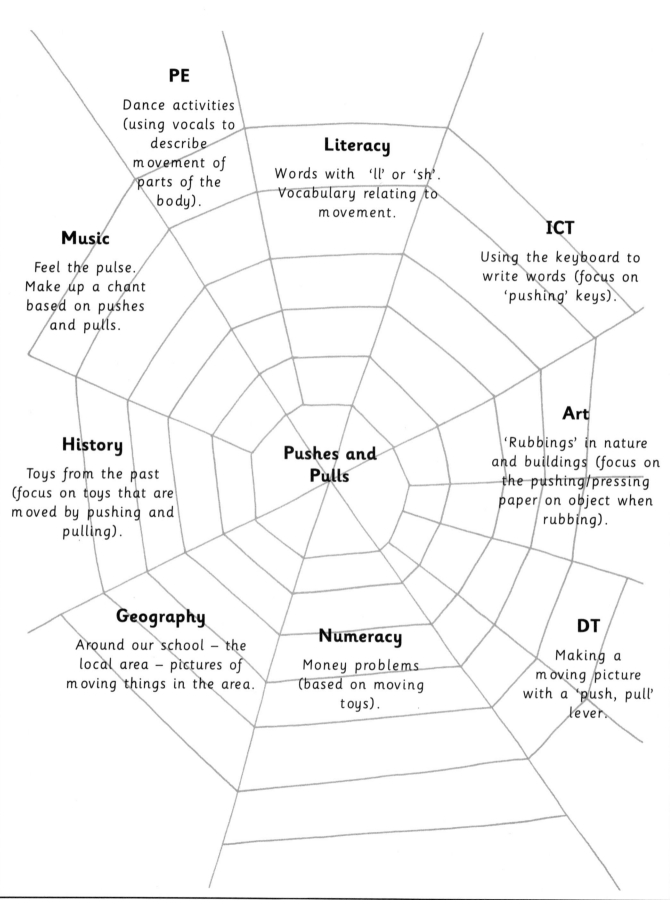

PE

Dance activities (using vocals to describe movement of parts of the body).

Literacy

Words with 'll' or 'sh'. Vocabulary relating to movement.

ICT

Using the keyboard to write words (focus on 'pushing' keys).

Music

Feel the pulse. Make up a chant based on pushes and pulls.

Art

'Rubbings' in nature and buildings (focus on the pushing/pressing paper on object when rubbing).

History

Toys from the past (focus on toys that are moved by pushing and pulling).

Pushes and Pulls

Geography

Around our school – the local area – pictures of moving things in the area.

Numeracy

Money problems (based on moving toys).

DT

Making a moving picture with a 'push, pull' lever.

Worksheet 1 contains a simple labelling activity, but one which requires children to distinguish between pushing and pulling.

Worksheet 2 shows a poem that features both pushing and pulling. It provides opportunities for children to consider everyday tasks that involve pushes or pulls. Worksheet 3 consists of comprehension questions, to be used as a literacy activity with some adult support. Some of the questions refer to 'push' and 'pull'.

Worksheet 4 includes vocabulary within a wordsearch. It includes many useful words needed to work on the 'Pushes and Pulls' unit.

Worksheets 5 and 6 are numeracy sheets containing questions linked to illustrated toys, though the main purpose of the sheet is to provide the opportunity to discuss the toys and how they move: Which ones are pulled? Which ones are pushed? How do the others move? We have provided a box at the foot of each page, to enable the children to record written or illustrated answers to the questions.

Worksheets 7, 8, and 9 – 'Look around owl/frog' have both been printed, to allow children some choice. The template will ideally be copied onto A4 card.
It is important for the vertical rectangles that hold the slider to be fixed, to allow the eyes to move from side to side but not too far up and down. Note: If children are positioned one side of the eyes and the slider is folded over rectangle B at the opposite side of the head, allowing only one end of the slider to be pushed or pulled, children are less likely to 'pull eyes' too far to one side. Encourage children to follow the instructions in the given order.

Worksheet 10 provides a chant for children to say together in a clear rhythmic way. Extra verses can be added just by asking the children to think of things that are 'pushed' or 'pulled'. When children are comfortable saying the chant they can be encouraged to clap or tap the beat. Children can also learn a simple set of actions to accompany the chant. While all children are chanting some can clap/tap the beat while others perform the actions:

Push, Pull Chant.

  c1   c   c2   c
Push the button, pull the string,

  c3   c   c   c
Push the wheelbarrow round and round.

  c1   c   c2   c
Push the button, pull the string,

  c2   c   c   c
Pull the rope that I have found.

  c1   c   c2   c
Push the button, pull the string,

  c4   c   c   c
Push the pedals round and round.

  c1   c   c2   c
Push the button, pull the string,

  c5   c   c   c
Pull the switch that I have found.

c = clap
1 = push air with both hands
2 = pull as if pulling on a rope
3 = push as in hands on wheelbarrow handles
4 = use one foot as if pedalling or two hands as if feet on pedals
5 = one hand, as if pulling 'bathroom' light switch

Name: | Date:

Push or pull?

Use the words **push** or **pull** to label the pictures.

The arrows will help you.

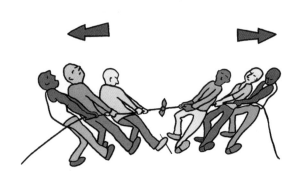

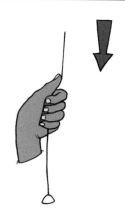

Name: Date:

Bedtime

Read the poem
carefully.

When I put my toys away
I push the door shut tight.
I'd hate my playthings to fall out
Onto the floor at night.

Then I climb into my bed
And pull the duvet round.
I snuggle in and close my eyes
Till dreamland I have found.

Now answer the questions on Worksheet 3.

Name: Date:

Bedtime

Put a ring round the correct answers.

● Circle the word from the poem, that rhymes with <u>tight</u>.

    fright   away   night   out

● Circle the word from the poem, that rhymes with <u>round</u>.

    bed   eyes   pound   found

● The title of the poem is -

    Toys   Bedtime   Dreamland

● What is being put away in a cupboard?

    toys   slippers   clothes   bed

● In the poem, what is being pushed?

    the bed   the door   the floor   the duvet

● In the poem, what is being pulled?

    the bed   the door   the floor   the duvet

Now carefully colour the illustrations on Worksheet 2

Name:

Date:

Wordsearch

Can you read the words in the box?

WORD BANK

push	pull	fast	slow
open	shut	twist	turn
jump	leap	hop	round
up	down		

Find the words in the wordsearch.

Colour each word as you find it.

The words might be written across ⟶ or downwards ↓ .

p	u	s	h	b	l	u	p	s	c	o	p	e	n
y	t	a	p	f	a	s	t	s	k	g	i	k	i
r	h	o	p	s	c	e	z	r	o	u	n	d	p
a	c	a	q	t	w	i	s	t	l	t	a	n	k
c	s	h	u	t	a	b	u	v	e	p	r	o	t
b	c	a	r	e	e	b	g	o	n	u	k	o	u
x	s	i	d	b	j	u	m	p	v	l	z	a	r
l	l	s	o	r	t	q	c	x	b	l	y	r	n
a	o	e	w	x	i	s	k	y	o	m	e	t	s
i	w	e	n	l	l	e	a	p	n	o	r	h	s

Name: Date:

Toys that move

Look at these toys. How do they move?

Each toy has a price label.

What can you buy with 10 pence?

Name: | Date:

Toys that move

Look at these toys. How do they move?

Each toy has a price label.

What can you buy with 20 pence?

Name: Date:

Look around owl/frog

Instructions:

- Carefully colour the owl or the frog picture.

- Cut it out along the dotted lines.

- Then cut out the three rectangles marked A and B.

- Cut out the eyes on the owl or the frog around the dotted lines. You may need an adult to help you with this.

- Fix the rectangles marked B into position on the back of the picture, on each side of the eyes. The diagram below will help you see what to do. Allow enough space for rectangle A to slide through the middle.

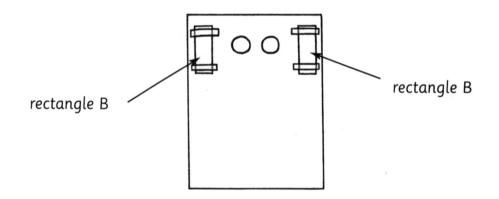

rectangle B   rectangle B

- Slide in rectangle A so that the eyes can be seen.

- Push or pull rectangle A to make your animal look from side to side.

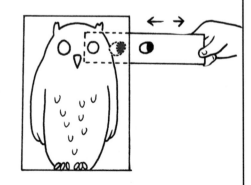

Andrew Brodie Publications © A & C Black Publishers Ltd

Name: | Date:

Look around owl

A

B | B

Name: Date:

Look around frog

A

B   B

Push, Pull Chant

Push the button, pull the string,
Push the wheelbarrow round and round.
Push the button, pull the string,
Pull the rope that I have found.

Push the button, pull the string,
Push the pedals round and round.
Push the button, pull the string,
Pull the switch that I have found.

We show possible curriculum links but we will not have thought of everything so you may like to add some of your own.

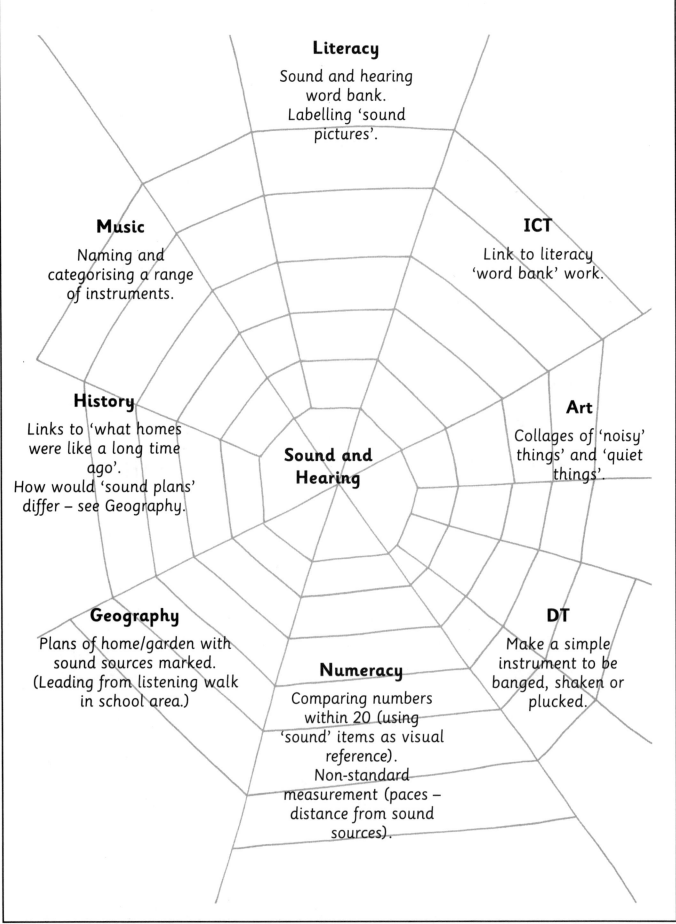

Literacy
Sound and hearing word bank.
Labelling 'sound pictures'.

Music
Naming and categorising a range of instruments.

ICT
Link to literacy 'word bank' work.

History
Links to 'what homes were like a long time ago'.
How would 'sound plans' differ – see Geography.

Art
Collages of 'noisy' things' and 'quiet things'.

Sound and Hearing

Geography
Plans of home/garden with sound sources marked.
(Leading from listening walk in school area.)

Numeracy
Comparing numbers within 20 (using 'sound' items as visual reference).
Non-standard measurement (paces – distance from sound sources).

DT
Make a simple instrument to be banged, shaken or plucked.

Worksheet 1 provides a range of vocabulary related to the theme of sound and hearing.

Worksheet 2 includes full sentences to be read by the children as part of their sentence level work for literacy.

Worksheets 3 and 4 are numeracy based sheets, but provide opportunities for discussion of musical instruments and how they make their sounds.

Worksheet 5 contains an investigation that could be completed by an individual or very small group working with an adult. The adult needs to collect several items for making sounds: a bell, a whistle, a maraca and a buzzer. Each child could be asked to face away from the adult or to cover her eyes, then to raise a hand when she hears the sound. Each time she hears the sound correctly, she should take one more step; then the adult repeats the sound. This continues until she no longer hears the sound and at that point the number of steps should be entered on the chart. If a child appears to fail to hear at a very early stage for each sound, it may be appropriate to report this to the class teacher and to the Special Needs Coordinator as the child may have some hearing loss.

Worksheet 6 shows a variety of musical instruments to be identified and to be classified according to the method of making sounds.

Worksheet 7 is a listening map on which children identify sounds and their sources at home. Similar activities could be centred around a school, a street or a sports centre.

Here are some ideas for other activities concerning sound and hearing in other curriculum areas:

Music – Using any rhyme or simple song known to the children, sing or say it in a variety of ways, e.g. loudly, quietly, whispering, high pitched, low pitched, squeakily, growling, etc. Encourage children to think of ways to do this.

P.E./Dance – Let children listen to different types and volumes of music as a starting point for creative movement. 'The Planets' by Gustav Holst is a good example of readily available music, that has examples of varying dynamics, speed, etc.

Art – Use pictures from magazines of things that make a noise and things that are silent. Ask children to choose a category of picture from which to make a collage. Extension: Ask children to select pictures that have items with a particular type of sound depicted on them, for example animal sounds, loud sounds, quiet sounds, rhythm sounds. Children will prove to be quite inventive in choosing their own categories.

Name: Date:

Noisy word search

- Find words from the box in the 'ear' below.

- Colour each word as you find it.

- Words may be written across → or downwards ↓ .

WORD BANK

silent   quiet   loud

noise   volume

shout   whisper   yell

roar   scream

Write the words.

```
a n l k z
s i l e n t x
r o a r s h q y
p d w q e d u j
o l y e l l i b
u v o l u m e p
n r i q x w t s
b w m z r h i q
n o i s e i t n
j s a c l s v d
z h e r o p k n
c o b e u e v
  u r a d r
  t j m o n
```

_____

_____

_____

_____

_____

_____

_____

_____

_____

_____

Andrew Brodie Publications © A & C Black Publishers Ltd.

SOUND AND HEARING

Literacy

2

Date:

Describing noises

Choose the label that goes with each picture.
Cut out the label and stick it in place.

The lion
roared loudly.

The noisy dog
barked and barked.

The teacher blew
the loud whistle.

The snow
fell silently.

The clock
ticked quietly.

Name:	Date:

Differences

Look at these pictures of 'noisy' items.

● How many more guitars than drums are there?

_____

● How many more triangles than tambourines are there?

_____

● How many more recorders than triangles are there?

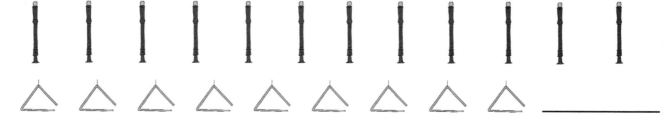

_____

● How many more drums than trumpets are there?

_____

● How many more guitars than tambourines are there?

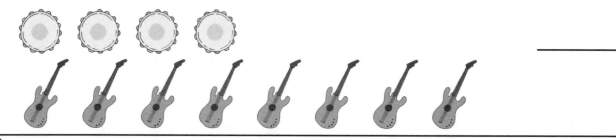

_____

Name: Date:

Differences

How many more trumpets than recorders are there?

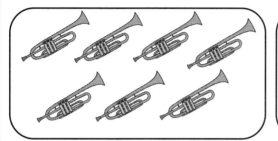 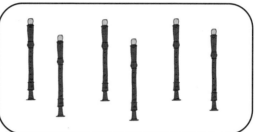 _____

How many more drums than guitars are there?

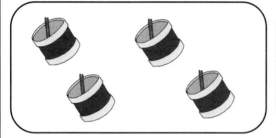  _____

How many more tambourines than triangles are there?

 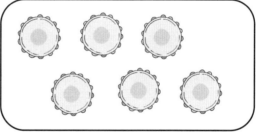 _____

How many more recorders than drums are there?

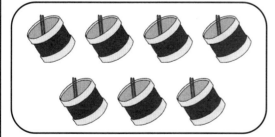  _____

How many more guitars than triangles are there?

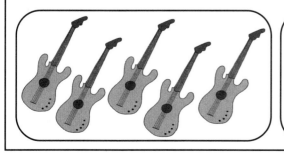 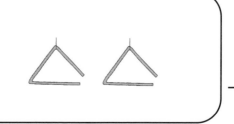 _____

Name: | Date:

Hearing sounds

Sounds seem quieter as you move further away from them.

If you move far enough away you cannot hear them at all.

Work with a partner.

See how many paces (steps) you can move from these sounds.

Stop when you can no longer hear the sound.

Sound	Number of steps at which the sound is no longer heard
whisper	
hum	
bell or whistle	
small toy falling	
maraca being shaken	
small buzzer	
hands clapping	

Name: Date:

Shake, hit or blow?

- Look at the pictures of musical instruments below.
- What sort of sounds do you think they make?
- Write the correct name below each picture.
- The names are in the box.
- Colour <u>green</u> the instruments that are blown to make a sound.
- Colour <u>blue</u> the instruments that are hit to make a sound.
- Colour <u>red</u> the instruments that are shaken to make a sound.

WORD BANK

recorder   claves

saxophone

maracas   drum

tambourine

_____

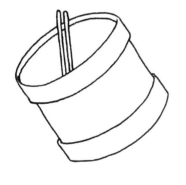

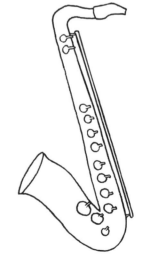

_____

_____

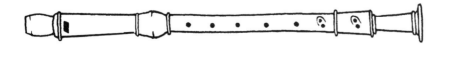

_____

_____

Name: Date:

My Home – a listening map

Draw the items in your house, garden and shed that make a noise.

Don't forget that televisions and computers are noisy.

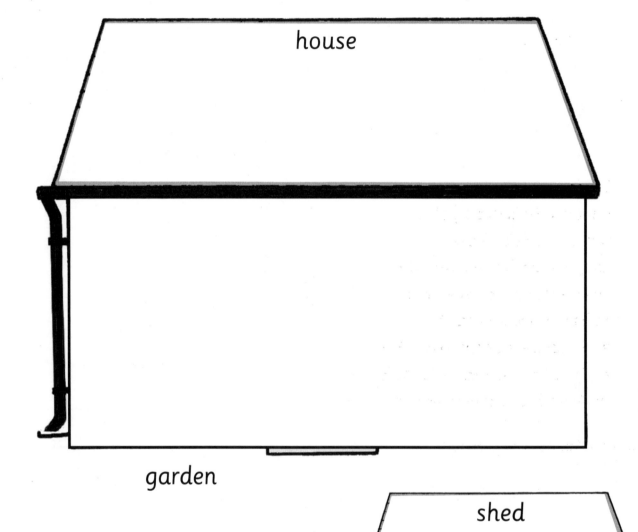

house

garden

shed